ABOUT

RUBY L. RADFORD  S0-EAR-524,
Georgia, and has lived there all her life. After
graduating from Teachers Training School in
her hometown, she studied short story and
fiction writing at Columbia University in New
York. She then taught art and history for eight
years, before resigning to devote full time to
writing.

Miss Radford has authored more than fifty
books, most of them for young people. She has
also had several hundred stories published in
children's magazines, many of which have
been included in school anthologies. Two have
been filmed for television use, others have been
on radio, put into braille, and taped for the
blind.

ABOUT THE ARTIST

JIM FOX is a graduate of Fordham University
and a former art student at the Cincinnati
Museum and the American School at Fontaine-
bleau, France. He has won fine arts awards
at the Columbia University Religious Arts
Exhibits, the Mount Kisco Junior League
Show, and the Chappaqua Open Air Arts
Exhibits. Mr. Fox has traveled widely in the
United States, Europe, and the Far East. He
lives with his family in Chappaqua, New York.

Inventors In Industry

Inventors

JULIAN MESSNER NEW YORK

In Industry

by Ruby L. Radford

Illustrated by Jim Fox

Published simultaneously in the United States and Canada by
Julian Messner, a division of Simon & Schuster, Inc.,
1 West 39 Street, New York, N.Y. 10018. All rights reserved.

Copyright, ©, 1969 by Ruby L. Radford
Printed in the United States of America
SBN 671-32181-1 Cloth Trade
671-32182-x MCE
Library of Congress Catalog Card No. 72-85406

Designed by Paula Wiener
and Leon Kotkofsky

In appreciation for their assistance
in researching my books, this collection of
biographies is dedicated to the librarians
of the Augusta-Richmond County Public Library:

Miss Frances Blackmon
Mrs. T. D. deTreville
Mrs. Carl Groover
Mrs. Sammie Lackey
Miss Dorothy Richey
Mrs. Barbara Symms

Contents

Inventors In Industry

Foreword

The Era of Industrial Progress in America

UNTIL THE END of the 1700's, men and horses worked America's farms to produce food. People made clothing and furniture by hand, often in their own homes. Compared with today's methods of farming and manufacturing, these were primitive ways. Then, in 1793, Eli Whitney invented the cotton gin. Farming and manufacturing began to change as, during the 1800's, other inventions were developed. The era of industrial progress in America was under way.

This book tells the stories of five inventors who helped change horsepower to electric power, and hand-crafting of goods at home to machine production of goods in factories. The five men in this collection had rare qualities that helped them to succeed. The most important was creative imagination. They saw a need for new products and figured out a way to fulfill that need. These men also had the willpower to carry a project through to perfection, despite the scorn of a skeptical public that would later profit by their sacrifices. They had one-track minds that could focus on a problem, brushing other matters aside. Finally, wives and families often encouraged these men in their work.

By the late 1800's, the bitter struggle of the lone, starving inventor became a thing of the past. In 1876, Thomas Edison established the first industrial laboratory, where assistant scientists and chemists helped him in his work. Today, no inventor need work alone. There are many industrial laboratories where his abilities will be welcomed and encouraged, in the hope that he—like these five men—will make an important contribution to American life.

R.L.R.

ONE

Eli Whitney

Inventor of the Cotton Gin

ELI WHITNEY was ten years old, and he sat playing with his father's big pocket watch. He wondered what kind of machinery made the hands of the watch move and keep time. He put the watch in his pocket and walked out of the farm house. Down the road, his father had a little workshop filled with all sorts of tools. There, Eli could take the watch apart and see how it worked.

The workshop was the place Eli loved best of all the places on the farm. He walked inside and looked around at the different kinds of tools, the stacks of wood, and the big lathe. His father used all this equipment to make furniture and repair wagons and plows.

Eli sat down with the watch and a screwdriver. Carefully, he took the watch apart. He noticed just how the gears fitted together. He laid the parts out in a row, all in order. Then, his curiosity satisfied, he put the watch back together and returned to the house. Someday this talent with machinery would take Eli Whitney far beyond the small workshop on the farm.

Eli Whitney was born on December 8, 1765, in the little town of Westborough, Massachusetts. He was named after his father, a farmer. Mr. Whitney was a big man, weighing nearly three hundred pounds. Eli, his eldest son, was larger than the average baby and the pride of his parents. Later, Mr. Whitney and his wife Elizabeth had three other children: Elizabeth, Benjamin, and Josiah.

As Eli grew up, his sister Elizabeth adored him. When she was grown, she wrote of his childhood: "He was remarkable for thinking and acting for himself at the age of ten or twelve years."

Eli learned how to make and repair farm implements, and sometimes he made pots and pans for his mother. A blacksmith nearby often let him use his forge to heat metal and shape it into tools. Eli was not happy when

14

he had to go to school. He much preferred puttering around the workshop and visiting the blacksmith.

Eli often had to help with the housework, for his mother became an invalid. Then, when he was about twelve, she died. Two years later, his father married a woman who had two daughters of her own. Eli did not like his stepmother very much; he thought she was always nagging him. So he spent more time than ever in the workshop.

Those were hard days for most people living in the American colonies. In 1776, when Eli was eleven, the Declaration of Independence had been signed. Men had begun to leave their homes to join in the war for freedom from England. Many products that had been shipped to the colonies from the "mother country" could no longer be bought. One of these scarce items was nails. Eli saw the chance to fill this need and to make some money, too. At the blacksmith shop, he learned to make nails.

One day he proudly showed his father some nails he had made. "If we had a forge in our workshop," he said, "I could make nails to sell."

So Mr. Whitney bought a forge, and Eli started a small nail business. He did so well that he had to hire a helper. But when the Revolutionary War ended in 1783, nails could again be bought from England. So Eli went out of business.

However, he was learning to adjust to changing times. Since he could no longer sell nails, he made walk-

Young Eli Whitney forging nails.

ing canes for men and hatpins for ladies, who no longer tied their bonnets under their chins.

When Eli was in his late teens, he decided there was no future in just being a handyman. He planned to become a lawyer. But a lawyer had to have a good education. At the supper table one evening he told his father he wanted to go to Leister Academy near his home.

His stepmother glared at him and said, "You have enough education for a farmer."

"I'm going to be a lawyer," stated Eli quietly, but firmly.

"I'm afraid that will cost too much, son," said his father. "We have many mouths to feed."

Realizing he would have to pay his own way, Eli got a teaching position. He earned seven dollars a month, plus meals. He saved most of what he earned to pay for a summer course at Leister Academy. For three years he taught in the winter and went to the academy in the summer.

The one-room school he taught in was not very comfortable. The children sat on backless benches, and only those who sat near the fireplace could keep warm. Whitney had to get up before daylight to tramp through the snow, build the fire, and clean the schoolroom. He taught reading, writing, spelling, and figuring to all the grades. He even showed his pupils how to make their own goose-quill pens and mix their own ink.

At the end of three years, he had worked so hard that he got very sick. During Eli's long illness at home, his father realized that he had worked too hard trying to save money for college. So Mr. Whitney promised to give Eli a thousand dollars for his education.

Eli Whitney was twenty-three when he entered Yale College in New Haven, Connecticut. Yale was only a small school then. President Ezra Stiles was helped by one professor and three tutors. The president discovered Whitney was a mechanical genius when he repaired a fragile instrument that had been broken in shipment from England.

In addition to studying hard, Whitney had to earn money to help pay his expenses, for his father's help was never quite enough. He did odd jobs for other students—coloring maps and mending shoes. He graduated from Yale in 1792 at the age of twenty-seven.

Though Whitney still liked to tinker with tools, he felt he could make a better living as a lawyer. With courage and determination, he knew he could find a way to finish his studies. He decided to teach while studying law at night. Through the help of Phineas

Miller, a former student at Yale, Whitney obtained a job in South Carolina, tutoring some children.

He sailed for the South with Miller and Mrs. Catherine Greene, the widow of the famous Revolutionary War hero, General Nathanael Greene. Miller was overseer on her plantation, Mulberry Grove, in Georgia. On the long journey to the port of Savannah, the three became good friends.

Soon after their arrival, Whitney learned that the teaching position in South Carolina would not pay as much as he expected. He refused to accept it. Mrs. Greene invited him to be her guest at Mulberry Grove before returning North. There, for the first time, he saw cotton growing.

Inland southern farmers raised their own cotton, tobacco, rice, vegetables, and cattle, but they had no crops big enough to sell for cash. They could have grown and sold a lot of short-fiber cotton, but they could not clean it fast enough. Cotton grows in fluffy white balls which have many tiny seeds sticking in them. It took one person a whole day to pick the seeds out of a pound of short-fiber cotton. So most farmers in middle and north Georgia and South Carolina were poor.

On the coast islands, however, farmers raised long-

Worker gathering cotton in the South.

fiber, or sea-island, cotton. Its seeds were very slippery and could be easily removed from the cotton. Plantation owners along the coast were growing rich on this long-fiber cotton. But it did not grow well inland.

One evening, Whitney met some farmers who were Mrs. Greene's dinner guests. They began talking about the problems of cleaning the seeds from short-fiber cotton. It was hard, slow work to separate the sticky green-coated seed from the cotton fiber. One farmer said to Whitney, "Only short-staple cotton will grow in this part of the country. If we had some easy way to seed it, we could make money on cotton, too."

When Mrs. Greene's guests were gone, she said to Whitney, "I believe you could make a machine to seed cotton."

She knew he was good at making and fixing machinery. He had repaired her broken watch during their sea voyage. And after coming to Mulberry Grove, he had made her some embroidery hoops and repaired farm tools. Whitney was delighted by her suggestion.

"I'll see what I can do to help the farmers," he said.

He drew some plans for a machine to clean seed from cotton. Phineas Miller helped him set up a workshop in the basement. In great secrecy, Whitney worked on his machine. At the end of the month, he had a crude working model. He and Miller became more and more excited over the idea. They agreed to form a partnership. Miller would furnish money for material and labor, while Eli would direct the work. However, the machine still needed many improvements. Whitney worked day after day in his basement workshop.

Finally, on September 11, 1793, Whitney wrote to his father: "The machine may be turned by water or horse power with the greatest ease. . . . It makes the labour fifty times less, without throwing any class of people out of business."

The machine was called the cotton engine, or cotton "gin."

Farmers had no cash to pay for ginning, so Miller and Whitney planned to charge two fifths of the cotton

Whitney demonstrates his cotton gin.

ginned as pay. Mrs. Greene invited some farmers to Mulberry Grove to see how the cotton gin worked. They could scarcely believe what they saw as Whitney turned the hand crank and Miller pushed seed cotton into the hopper. Metal teeth pulled the cotton through slits too narrow to let the seed through. Inside, a brush cleaned the cotton lint from the turning cylinder and pushed the cotton out the other side, free of seed.

One delighted farmer exclaimed, "This is the greatest invention ever made!"

"We can now raise enough cotton to ship North and to England," said another. "We'll be as rich as the sea-island planters."

Soon, four cotton gins were operating at Mulberry Grove and several others in Georgia and South Carolina. Everyone was excited and curious about the new machinery. Whitney tried to keep secret how he had made it, for fear someone would steal his idea.

He returned to New Haven to build a shop, hire workmen, and get material to make more cotton gins. He applied to Thomas Jefferson, the Secretary of State, for a patent to protect his right to the idea of the cotton gin and to keep anyone from stealing the idea. His patent was dated March 14, 1794, and signed by President George Washington.

While Whitney was making more gins in New Haven, disturbing news came from Miller. Several planters had copied Whitney's machine and were ginning cotton on their own plantations. Miller and Whitney asked the courts to make these planters stop using Whitney's idea. But the Georgia courts upheld the farmers, who claimed that Miller and Whitney were charging too much for ginning and that any planter had right to such an invention. Whitney's patent gave him no real protection.

In the spring of 1795, while Whitney was ill with malaria, his shop burned down and all his machinery was ruined. Still, he could not give up. With the determination he had always shown, he rebuilt his shop, better than before. Seven months later he had twenty-seven cotton gins ready to ship South.

That spring, Yale College honored him by giving him the degree of Master of Arts for his invention. But Whitney's troubles were not over. He and Miller were deeply in debt. They had to sue more and more planters who had copied Whitney's cotton gin. The company would have failed had not Mrs. Greene given them financial backing.

During the struggle for his rights to the gin, Whitney made six trips South. Expenses were so great that he made little profit from his invention. Not until 1802 did the Georgia courts finally rule that Whitney was the real inventor of the cotton gin. By that time his patent had expired, and gins made by others were operating all over the South.

However, the invention of the cotton gin gave a great boost to the economy of the South. Within five years after gins started operating, cotton raised in the South increased from three million pounds to eleven million. Northern cotton mills profited, too, because there was plenty of cotton to weave into cloth. The new industrial era had begun.

Once more, Eli Whitney had to find a new way to make a living. He had given up the idea of becoming a lawyer, but he had learned that a handyman could do important work.

At that time, the United States badly needed guns. It had been buying guns in England; but then England went to war with France and needed all its guns. Once again, Whitney spotted an opportunity. Up to that time, guns had been made by hand. Whitney thought he could build machines to make guns as he had built machines to make cotton gins. He believed guns could be made faster and better by machines.

Whitney's plan was this. He would build a different

machine to make each part of a gun. Each worker in his factory would be trained to operate one machine and make one kind of part. That way, every gun barrel would be like every other barrel, and every gunlock would be like every other. Then the various parts could be assembled, put together with screws, so that all the guns would be exactly alike. This was a new idea in manufacturing.

Eli wrote about his plan to Oliver Wolcott, Secretary of the Treasury, at the national capital in Philadelphia. The government liked his idea and hired him to make ten thousand guns, for which he would be paid $134,000. Whitney was expected to deliver four thousand guns within twenty-eight months. He was given an advance of $5,000 to begin work.

Whitney had a big job ahead. He had to hire workmen and find a place on a stream where his machinery could be run by water power. He had to buy iron ore and other materials. He was so busy he rarely had time to visit his family, but he kept in touch with them by letter. His sister Elizabeth had married and had sons. Though Eli was now thirty-two, he was still unmarried and had to face his problems and disappointments alone.

At his gun factory in Mill Rock, Connecticut, he

had more difficulties to overcome. Winter snows and ice delayed work on the factory. The ground was frozen so hard that iron ore could not be mined. The following summer some of the workmen fell ill with yellow fever.

At the end of the twenty-eight months, when Whitney was expected to deliver four thousand guns, he had none ready. It had taken much longer than he expected to build his factory and machinery. To make matters worse, he had spent all the money advanced him. Desperately, he wrote to Wolcott, asking for more money and more time to make the guns.

Secretary Wolcott replied that he still had faith in Whitney's idea. He advanced Whitney $1,500 more to continue his work. This amount was still not enough, so Wolcott promised to send an additional $10,000 if ten New Haven citizens would also sign the loan papers. Whitney had many friends who believed in his work and agreed to back him. After that, he continued his work with more confidence.

In spite of this financial help, Whitney could not get the guns finished on time. The government grew impatient and asked him to come to Washington, now the new capital, to explain how he had spent all the money. Whitney had plenty of gun parts finished, but none put together for delivery. He packed many of these different gun parts into a big chest and took a stagecoach to Washington.

Whitney met with a group of officials in a large room in one of the government buildings. Army officers were there, dressed in their blue uniforms. Even the President, John Adams, was there waiting to hear Whitney's explanation. Whitney felt a bit more comfortable when he saw the friendly faces of Secretary Wolcott and Thomas Jefferson. Whitney and Jefferson had exchanged several letters after Jefferson gave Whitney a patent on his cotton gin. As a Virginia farmer as well as a government official, Jefferson appreciated what the cotton gin had done for the South. Now, he had faith in Whitney's new idea for manufacturing guns. But the others were doubtful, thinking that perhaps Whitney had already wasted too much of the government's money.

On a long table, Whitney spread out his gun parts. Then he asked one of the army officers to hand him the parts needed to make one gun. With only a screwdriver and screws, Whitney quickly assembled a gun. As he worked, he explained that by making every gun part with machinery, the parts would be interchange-

Before a group of officials, Whitney assembles a gun using his interchangeable parts.

able, and so a gun could be put together quickly. After that, repairs would be simple; uniform parts could be ordered from the factory.

This way of manufacturing was entirely new. No one had ever seen a gun put together so quickly and perfectly. The government officials realized that Whitney's streamlined methods not only would produce excellent guns, but would improve manufacturing all over the country. As a result, the delivery date for the guns was extended, and more money was advanced to Whitney.

After that, Eli Whitney's success was assured. There were still many problems to solve and much work to be done, but at least he could go ahead with the assurance of government backing. To keep his trained workers on the job, he built stone homes for them near the factory. He even had a boarding house for the unmarried men. This first factory town was called Whitneyville.

For many years the government continued to give Whitney orders for guns. When war with England came in 1812, his factory produced more guns than ever. By that time, he was a prosperous man.

Whitney was fifty-one when he finally married Henrietta Edwards, granddaughter of the famous

preacher Jonathan Edwards. They had two daughters, Frances and Elizabeth, and a son, Eli Whitney, Jr.

When Whitney's health began to fail, his sister's son, Eli Blake, took charge of the gun factory. Whitney had sent this nephew to Yale and later taught him the business. After only eight years of happy married life, Whitney died on January 8, 1825.

When Eli Whitney, Jr. was grown he took over his father's business. It remained in the Whitney family for ninety years, then was sold to Winchester Arms.

Eli Whitney's invention of the cotton gin and his methods of mass production began a new agricultural and industrial era. The United States was soon producing more cotton than any other country in the world, while factories all over the nation were using Whitney's method of mass production by machinery. Eli Whitney, the handyman, had started his country on the way to great agricultural and industrial wealth.

TWO

Cyrus Hall McCormick

Inventor of the Reaper

WHEAT HAS BEEN a basic food for many centuries, for many civilizations all over the world. But until the nineteenth century, farmers could not harvest wheat very quickly. So they could grow only as much wheat as they could harvest by hand. Then the reaper was invented by Cyrus Hall McCormick, who was born on Walnut Grove Farm, in a valley of Virginia's Blue Ridge Mountains, on February 13, 1809.

As soon as he was old enough to swing a scythe—a curved blade on a curved handle—Cyrus helped his father cut wheat in the fields. But in winter he went to the log country schoolhouse nearby with his younger brothers, Leander and William. Their mother, Mary Ann, wove cloth called homespun and sewed it into clothes for the family. On Sundays, the McCormicks went to the Presbyterian church, just like their Scotch-Irish ancestors, who had settled in Pennsylvania in 1734. Cyrus's great-grandfather, Thomas McCormick, had fought the Indians, and his grandfather had helped win American independence during the Revolution.

Cyrus's father, Robert McCormick, a farmer and inventor, had moved to Virginia. He had built an improved plow to till the hillside fields, and invented other farm tools. Then he started work on a grain reaper that would cut stalks of wheat mechanically. A farmer could not harvest much grain with a scythe.

Using a scythe, Cyrus helps his father cut wheat.

He had to swing the scythe by hand. The grain heads had to be held upright and then bundled into sheaths. It was hard, slow work. Even the best reapers could cut only an acre of grain in a day. Then the grain was threshed from the stalks, and the chaff was winnowed —cleaned from the grain.

Mr. McCormick could raise plenty of wheat on his eighteen hundred acres of farmland. But he had a problem—all his wheat ripened at about the same time. Even in fair weather, he could not hire enough workers to help his family, servants, and slaves gather the wheat before too much of the golden grain fell to the ground and rotted. He did well if he harvested enough for his family and occasionally a little to sell.

For many years, he continued working on a machine to harvest wheat. When neighbors dropped into his blacksmith shop, they laughed at his idea. They said Robert McCormick was a dreamer and wasting his time. Other people had tried to make reapers and had failed. But young Cyrus believed it could be done as he watched his father at work.

By the time Cyrus was ten, he was a tall, sturdy boy, and could use many of the tools in the blacksmith shop. Jo Anderson, one of the McCormick slaves, was also a good blacksmith and helped teach Cyrus how to work with tools. Cyrus liked best to work at the forge and on the old stone anvil, where red-hot iron was shaped into horseshoes or cranes on which to hang pots in the open fireplace.

Like all growing farm boys, Cyrus had to help in the fields. The first time he harvested wheat, his back and arms ached from swinging the heavy scythe. With Jo's help he made a lighter scythe in the blacksmith shop. When he was in his teens, he improved his father's plow by making it turn the soil back. When he was twenty-one, he secured a government patent for this plow. He and his father made several and sold them at a profit.   .

Finally, Robert McCormick became discouraged about the reaper and stopped working on it. He had tried to build a machine that followed the motion of a man's arm swinging a scythe. But Cyrus had another idea—why not cut the wheat with scissor-like knives placed on a bar. This machine could be set on a low, horse-drawn platform with wheels. The wheat had to fall onto the platform with all the grain heads facing in the same direction, so that the grain could be gathered into sheaves. Cyrus began experimenting with this idea.

Several times his machine almost worked, but some-

With the help of Jo Anderson,
McCormick builds his first reaper.

thing went wrong. Cyrus had the persistence of his
Scotch-Irish ancestors, though. He tried again and
again. In July, 1831, when he was twenty-two, his
machine was finally ready—but not in time for the

harvest. However, his father left one field uncut until Cyrus had finished his reaper.

Cyrus brought out his reaper and hitched it to a horse. Jo Anderson drove it to the edge of the field of golden grain. With a great clatter the reaper moved and cut, dropping the ripe grain stalks onto the platform. Cyrus walked alongside, raking off the wheat to be gathered into sheaves.

Shouts of joy went up from the watching McCormick family. After all the years of effort, the reaper was a success at last. That night, around the supper table, the family offered thankful prayers.

"Cyrus, I believe your machine can do the work of six men," said his father gratefully.

"But it's still far from perfect," replied Cyrus. "I'll make more improvements before the next harvest. Then maybe I'll demonstrate it to other wheat growers."

During the winter, Cyrus made new parts to hold the wheat upright for cutting. He built an adjustable platform and improved the gearing. At harvest time, he took the reaper over to Lexington, eighteen miles away, for a demonstration. Curious farm families watched the strange contraption go down the dusty road.

When he reached the wheat field he was to cut, Cyrus began to feel doubtful. The field was rough and uneven, and his reaper worked much better on level land. But it was too late to back out. A boy mounted the horse that was hitched to the reaper and drove off with a deafening clatter to the edge of the field. Jo Anderson walked beside the platform to rake off the grain. Behind them strode the tall inventor, watching how his machine worked.

The field was so rough that the grain scattered. Some laborers began to jeer. They had always used scythes and were afraid the machine would take away their work.

Suddenly the owner of the field ran after Cyrus yelling, "You're ruining my wheat! Get that thing out of here!"

Cyrus was stunned. But a moment later, a farmer, who owned an adjoining wheat field that was on more level ground, offered to let the reaper cut his grain. Cyrus and the farmer tore down the split-rail fence that separated the fields. Then the reaper was driven through into the other field. Before sundown, the reaper had cut six acres of grain. The watching crowd felt as if they had seen a miracle.

"Why, Cyrus!" exclaimed a friend. "That machine's worth a hundred thousand dollars!"

Cyrus replied dryly, "I'd gladly take half that amount for it."

So curious and excited was everyone about the invention that Cyrus put the reaper on display in the courthouse square in Lexington.

The reaper had succeeded in its first public demonstration. But Cyrus wanted to make more improvements before he applied for a government patent to protect his right. In 1833, he was shocked to read in the paper that a man named Obed Hussey had secured a patent for a reaper. To protect his own invention, Cyrus secured his government patent the following year.

At the time, there seemed little hope of making a living on his invention, so Cyrus farmed some land his father gave him. He also went into business with his father, making and selling pig iron. There was plenty of iron ore in the Blue Ridge Mountains. A furnace was put in near the mine to melt out the ore. The McCormicks made money for a while. Then, in 1837, financial troubles struck most of the nation's businesses. The McCormicks, like many others, were wiped out.

McCormick demonstrates his reaper.

They had to give up half their land and even mortgage their home to pay their debts.

This trouble proved to be a blessing in disguise for Cyrus. Hoping he could make a reaper good enough to manufacture and sell, he went back to work in his shop at Walnut Grove. Though the basic structure of the machine stayed the same, he made several small improvements on it.

Finally, in 1840, he sold two reapers for one hundred dollars each. Seven were bought in 1842, twenty-nine the following year at three thousand dollars each, and fifty a year later. The improved McCormick reaper was on its way to success.

The Walnut Grove workshop had become too small to build as many machines as people wanted to buy. Cyrus and his brothers, Leander and William, who worked with him, decided it was time to build factories in other parts of the country.

So, in 1844, Cyrus mounted his horse and went on a three-thousand-mile journey through the Midwest. He looked for good places to build reaper factories, and he visited wheat growers on the plains. He knew his reaper would work well on such level land. Although many farmers wanted the reaper, they could not afford the price because they made so little money growing wheat that had to be harvested by hand.

Then Cyrus thought of a plan to help the wheat growers and at the same time boost his own sales. He would let the farmers buy reapers and pay for them over a period of time on an installment plan. With the reaper they could harvest more wheat and so make more money to pay for the reaper. Cyrus was warned that he would lose money by trusting people, but he went ahead anyway.

Another business method that helped sweep McCormick to success was securing written statements from pleased customers, and publishing them in the papers. This advertising made many people want to buy reapers. He also gave his customers written agreements that the reapers could be returned if they did not work well.

After his journey, Cyrus gave permission to two manufacturers, Seymour and Morgan, to make and sell McCormick reapers at Rockport, New York. The manufacturers agreed to pay him a percentage of the money they made. Then his brother Leander went to Cincinnati to build a reaper factory there.

While on his midwestern tour, Cyrus had gone as

far as Chicago, which was then only a small village on Lake Michigan. He realized that Chicago might someday become a great center of trade. The city's mayor, William G. Ogden, was so impressed with McCormick's reaper that he bought a half interest in the factory Cyrus built on the Chicago River in 1847. Before the next harvest, fifty thousand dollars' worth of reapers were sold. Later, Cyrus bought out Ogden's share of the business. After that, he kept all ownership within the family.

However, as business increased, troubles multiplied. By the time the McCormick patent had expired, Cyrus and Obed Hussey had fought several court battles over who was the real inventor of the reaper. More often than not, Cyrus lost the suits, but he continued to expand his business and sell more and more machines.

Finally, the patent office refused to renew McCormick's patent. It claimed that the reaper was too valuable to humanity for one person to own all the rights. Eventually, it was proved that Cyrus was the inventor, for he had demonstrated his reaper in 1831, before Hussey had secured his patent in 1833.

However, owning the patent did not protect McCormick. Several manufacturers had stolen his idea and were making and selling reapers. Yet, he did succeed, in spite of all this competition.

He had gone to the wheat growers and talked to them about their needs. He was one of the first manufacturers to use the installment plan. His factories used mass production, which Eli Whitney had begun with his cotton gin and gun manufacturing.

When the gold rush to California started in 1849, many families stopped to settle in the Midwest, where McCormick reapers made it possible for farmers to grow rich on golden grain. By 1851 McCormick was selling a thousand reapers a year.

McCormick spread his sales and advertising to Europe. In 1851, his reaper was displayed at the International Exhibition in England. Obed Hussey also exhibited his reaper. In the reaping contest between the two machines, McCormick's came out victorious. He was awarded the Council Medal, the highest prize of the Fair. The London *Times* wrote that the McCormick reaper was "worth the cost of the whole exhibition." At the International Exhibition in France in 1855 the McCormick reaper was given the Medal of Honor.

During the Civil War, the reaper freed thousands of men from field work to serve in the army. Secretary of War Edwin M. Stanton said, "Without McCormick's reaper, I fear the North could not win."

As a Virginian, McCormick's sympathies were with the South. But after the war he bought a newspaper, *The Inquirer*, and in it he wrote about reuniting Presbyterians of the North and South. Later, he founded the McCormick Theological Seminary in Chicago. His pastor said, "He thought of souls as well as machines."

Cyrus was fifty years old when he married the beautiful and brilliant Nettie Fowler of New York. She encouraged him in his work. When the Chicago fire of 1871 destroyed his factory, she convinced him to

The Chicago fire of 1871 destroys the McCormick reaper factory.

rebuild, even though he could have retired on the fortune he had made.

After McCormick's death in 1884, his son, Cyrus, Jr., was elected president of the McCormick Harvesting Company. In 1902, the business merged with several other companies that manufactured farm implements, and formed the International Harvester Company. In memory of Jo Anderson, who helped McCormick build his first reaper, this company has been a pioneer in equal and fair treatment of Negro employees.

Cyrus Hall McCormick was one of the few inventors who from childhood had a workshop where he developed his mechanical genius. Little did he dream, however, when he began working on his reaper in the old blacksmith shop at Walnut Grove, that in the twentieth century over two million reapers would be harvesting grain all over the world.

THREE

Elias Howe

Inventor of the Sewing Machine

ON A BRIGHT AFTERNOON in 1825 six-year old Elias Howe and his older brother, Amassa, hurried home from school. When they reached their father's grist mill, they stopped for a moment to watch the water tumbling over the big wheel. Then they ran on. Elias had been born on the family farm near Spencer, Massachusetts, on July 9, 1819. His father, Elias Howe, Sr., and his mother, Polly, also had a younger son and daughter.

Elias was a frail boy, with dark curly hair and merry eyes. As he and Amassa left the mill, he limped along beside his brother, for one leg was shorter than the other. He could not play running games with other boys, but he liked to work with his hands.

When the brothers reached home, they sat down at a work table in the shop. Every day after school, they helped their father make wire brushes to sell to the Lowell cotton mill. Elias began sticking the wires through a strip of leather, but Amassa looked longingly out the window. He preferred helping his father in the fields, for Mr. Howe had a farm as well as a grist mill.

"I like to make the brushes," said Elias, whose deft fingers could make them as fast as his older brother. He knew they were used for carding cotton, which was spun into thread at the mill.

As Elias grew older, he learned to use the hammer, saw, and awl, and to weld tin and copper. He spent many hours every day in the workshop. His pretty, curly-haired mother was proud of the teakettle he made for her.

Elias was delighted one day when his father took him to visit the Lowell cotton mill. He saw some of the wire brushes they had made, carding cotton that would be made into thread. In the roar of the weaving room, he watched the cotton thread being made into cloth. The big weaving machine seemed miraculous, as its shuttles carried the woof threads back and forth

Elias and his father visit the Lowell cotton mill.

through the warp threads stretched on the loom. Elias had watched his mother weave rugs by hand. Now, weaving was done much faster by machinery.

Elias thought of his mother patiently sewing clothes by hand. If she only had a sewing machine, how much more quickly she could do it, the boy thought. Why hadn't someone invented a sewing machine? Elias did not dream then that he would someday invent a sewing machine. He had years of school ahead of him. But he read everything he could find about inventors and inventions.

In those days, not many people went to college. When Elias finished school at sixteen, he and his best friend, George Fisher, took jobs in the Lowell mill. There, they learned to operate the newly invented carding machine. Later, they learned to put bobbins of thread into the shuttles that wove the cloth. The job in Lowell lasted only two years. Then the financial panic of 1837 forced the mill owners to close the mill and fire all the workers.

George went to work with his uncle, who was in the coal and wood business. Elias was hired for six dollars a week by Ari Davis, a watchmaker in Cambridge. Davis taught Elias to help him make scientific and surveying instruments for Harvard College. Many inventors came to the shop, and while Elias worked, he liked to listen to their talk. From them, he learned a great deal about machinery.

By the time Elias Howe was twenty-one, he was earning nine dollars a week. He decided to marry Elizabeth J. Ames of Boston. Elizabeth earned a little money by sewing clothes and selling them. In the evenings, Howe watched her sewing. There are so many inventions, he thought, but not much has been done to lighten women's work.

He began to think about a man he had met a few months before in Ari Davis's shop. The man had put a strange-looking instrument on the counter and said,

While Howe worked, he listened to the
talk of inventors who visited the Davis Shop.

"I'm trying to make a mechanical knitter, but it won't
work. Maybe you can tell me what's wrong."

Davis had examined the instrument, and then, shak-
ing his head, had answered, "Why don't you make a

sewing machine instead? It's needed more and would make you a fortune."

Howe decided to invent a sewing machine himself. First, he tried a machine that imitated the movements of a woman's hand as she used a needle. But that did not work. Next, he thought of using a double-pointed needle, with an eye in the middle. That idea failed, too. Then he tried putting the eye near the point. All this experimenting took time and money, for he had to buy steel and other materials.

Finally, he thought of using two threads—one on a spool and the other on a bobbin. He had seen that method used in weaving cloth. The needle, fed with thread from the spool, went down into the cloth and left a loop of thread. The shuttle, carrying the bobbin back and forth, put the second thread through the loop to hold the stitches firm. All these moving parts were operated by a hand-turned wheel.

It took Howe over three years to make that much progress. He could only work on his invention after long, tiring hours in Davis's shop. He and Elizabeth had three children by then. It was almost impossible for him to spare money to buy material for his machine.

He and his family moved in with his parents, who had moved to Cambridge. Howe set up a workshop in the attic. Still, his troubles were not over. He could not continue his work without materials. George Fisher, who had become a successful coal and wood dealer, heard of his friend Howe's troubles. He offered to take in the Howes. In return for a half interest in the invention, Fisher also advanced Howe five hundred dollars in cash.

Two years later, in April 1845, the Howe and Fisher families went up to the workshop to watch Howe sew two pieces of cloth together. After five years of hard effort, Elias Howe's sewing machine worked. The first thing he made on the machine was a suit of clothes for George Fisher. Then he made one for himself. The next step was to get people to buy his sewing machine.

The Quincy Clothing Manufacturing Company let Howe use a room in their factory to demonstrate it to the public. For two weeks, curious people watched Elias Howe sew pieces of cloth together, but no one wanted to buy a machine. Finally, Howe held a contest with five of the factory's best seamstresses. One cloth of equal length was given to each of the girls, while Elias had five pieces of cloth of the same length. He stitched all five on his machine before any of the hand experts had finished one.

Howe at his sewing machine holds a
sewing contest with five seamstresses.

Still, people were not convinced of the value of his invention. Seamstresses were afraid the fast machine would put them out of work. The factory claimed the cost of the machine was too high.

To protect the rights to his invention, Howe had to get a government patent. With George Fisher's financial help, he built a better machine. In the summer of 1846 Howe and Fisher went to Washington with this second machine. That patent was issued on September 10. That sewing machine may still be seen in the Smithsonian Institution in Washington, D. C.

Still, there were no buyers for the machine. George Fisher felt he had spent enough money on an invention that was a failure. He had taken care of Elias Howe's family for two years and advanced money for building the machines. He could no longer take care of them. Their agreement was canceled, and Howe moved his family back to his father's house. When his brother Amassa, who had become a sailor, was home on vacation, Elias discussed the problem of his sewing machine with him.

Amassa made a suggestion. "On my next visit to England," he said, "I could take the machine there and try to sell the rights."

Elias was delighted at the idea. He knew the Eng-

56

lish had invented many new kinds of machinery. Perhaps they would now be interested in his.

Mr. Howe lent his son enough money to build a third machine. In England, Amassa sold the rights to a corset manufacturer, William Thomas, for 250 pounds in English money. Thomas also wanted Howe to come to England and adapt the sewing machine for corset making. He promised to pay him nine dollars a week while he did the work.

On February 5, 1847, Elias and Amassa sailed for England. They traveled in steerage and cooked their own food on the long journey. Soon after Howe's arrival, Thomas advanced him money to bring his wife and children to England.

The move proved to be a sad mistake. The foggy climate of England made Elizabeth ill. Working conditions in Thomas's factory finally became unbearable for Howe, so he left the factory. In later years, Thomas did not keep his contract to pay Elias three pounds for every machine he sold. Eventually he made millions of dollars on Howe's invention.

Elizabeth became so ill that she had to leave England. Elias had so little money that he pawned some of his clothes to pay a hack to take her and the children to the ship. He stayed in England to finish his fourth machine, which he sold for four pounds. Then to pay his debts and his passage home, he pawned his first sewing machine and his patent papers. After being in England for two years, he left there a disappointed and penniless man.

He had barely reached home when Elizabeth died of tuberculosis. Howe felt that he had little to live for; he had lost his wife, and his life's work seemed to have been a failure.

Soon after his return from England, Howe learned that several people had used his idea and were making and selling sewing machines. One of these people was Isaac M. Singer, who had made some improvements on the machine.

Howe examined some of the machines Singer and others were selling. He found they all used the original idea he had invented. But he had no money to sue these people. Finally, a man named George Bliss helped him pay lawyers to sue Isaac Singer. Howe claimed he was owed royalties—payments from the sale of all machines using his patented idea. In 1854, the courts agreed, and said that Elias Howe was the real inventor of the sewing machine.

Singer was forced to operate under a Howe license, which meant that Howe would get royalties on every machine Singer sold. Singer also had to pay Howe $15,000 in royalties for previous sales. Eventually, Singer made many improvements on the sewing machine, and today many machines all over the world bear the Singer name.

Once the suits were settled, the Howe sewing machine went into factories and homes all over the world. In 1867, the Emperor Napoleon III of France awarded Howe the Cross of the Legion of Honor for his invention.

Howe died on October 3, 1872, at his daughter's home in Brooklyn, New York. His estate was then valued at thirteen million dollars.

Elias Howe's invention of the sewing machine not only made women's work easier, it contributed much to the progress of American industry. It led to the development of many kinds of sewing machines for making clothes in large quantities in factories. Shoes, pocketbooks, mattresses, and many other products also are made by sewing machines. Thousands of people are now employed in all these industries. In appreciation for his great invention, a statue of Elias Howe has been placed in the Hall of Fame in Washington, D. C.

FOUR

Charles Goodyear
Inventor of Vulcanized Rubber

WHEN COLUMBUS landed in the Western Hemisphere, he found Indian children playing with black, bouncy balls. They were made from the gum of a tropical tree. Columbus took some of the sticky substance back to Spain, but no one paid attention to it. In the late 1700's, someone discovered it would rub out pencil marks. So the black gum was called India rubber, for it was thought Columbus had brought it from India.

For three hundred years, people tried to make use of rubber, but it became soft and sticky in summer, hard and brittle in winter. It was not until 1839 that one man found a way to make rubber gum into a useful product. That man was Charles Goodyear.

Goodyear was born on December 19, 1800, in New Haven, Connecticut. His parents, Cynthia and Amassa Goodyear, were descendants of original settlers of New Haven. Mr. Goodyear was a manufacturer of farm implements. He had also invented and patented several new tools. The most profitable had been a steel pitchfork.

In his youth, Charles wanted to be a Congregational minister, but his father could not afford to send him to school after he was seventeen. So Charles was apprenticed to Rogers & Brothers, hardware dealers in Philadelphia.

When Charles completed his apprenticeship on his twenty-first birthday, he returned home and went into partnership with his father. Three years later, he married Clarissa Beecher of New Haven. The business did so well during the next two years that the Goodyears decided to open a retail hardware store in Philadelphia, with Charles in charge. His brother Robert joined the firm which was called A. Goodyear and Sons.

The friendly Charles gave too much credit and could not always collect what people owed him. When

Charles selling in the family hardware store.

the financial crash of 1830 forced the store to close, Charles decided he would repay the firm's $30,000 debt. He did not want the business to go bankrupt, for fear his father would lose the income from the sales of tools he had invented.

Soon, Charles Goodyear and his wife and children scarcely had enough to eat. Nor was there any money to pay back the debts. Clarissa helped a little by spinning linen thread to sell.

When Goodyear could not find work in Philadelphia, he left his family there and went to New York.

62

After a discouraging day hunting for a job, he stopped to look in the show window of the Roxbury India Rubber Company. He had read in the paper how someone had combined rubber gum with chemicals and used it to waterproof boots, coats, life preservers, and other articles.

Eagerly Goodyear went into the store and asked to examine the life preserver. But it would not inflate when he tried to blow it up.

"This life preserver has a faulty valve," he said. "I'm sure I can make a better one."

He was interested in more than the valve, however. He also wanted to know more about the rubber itself. Though his children needed food, he bought the life preserver. All their future might be brighter, he thought, if he could make and sell a successful life preserver, and perhaps other rubber products.

Back in Philadelphia, he made a better valve and inflated the tube. Hoping to sell the improved valve to the Roxbury company, he returned to New York on a hot summer day. But the manager of the store was not interested.

"The better valve will do us no good now," he said. "This heat has turned all my rubber goods into a soft, sticky mess."

He showed Goodyear the ruined overshoes, coats, and life preservers.

"If anyone can find a way to keep rubber goods from becoming soft and sticky in summer and brittle in winter, he will make a fortune," said the manager.

From that moment, Charles Goodyear determined he would discover that process. He knew little about chemistry, but he thought he could learn by trial and error, as he experimented. He bought some cheap rubber gum and set up a makeshift laboratory in his kitchen. First, he melted some rubber, then added turpentine, and rolled the mess out on his wife's breadboard. The family watched eagerly as he started his work.

Goodyear experiments in the family kitchen.

Goodyear hoped he could earn money by finding a way to make serviceable rubber, for his debtors were demanding payment. In those days, a man could be arrested if he could not pay his debts. But his debtors grew tired of waiting for their money while Goodyear melted rubber in his kitchen. They had him thrown into prison.

Hard times had struck the Goodyear family more harshly than ever. Goodyear became ill on the prison food. Clarissa had to sell some of her wedding linen to buy food for the children. But she still believed in her husband's idea, and she spent some of the money she earned to buy raw rubber and chemicals so Charles could experiment in prison. The jailer was kind enough to let him work at a table and stove.

While he was still in prison, Charles invented a new farm tool. It brought enough money to pay some of his debts, so he was released.

A boyhood friend lent him money, and for the next year he continued his experiments. Clarissa and the older children helped him cover boots, sheets, and coats with the waterproof rubber. Then these articles were stored away. The family waited to see how the waterproofing stood changes in the weather.

One hot day Clarissa opened the storage-room door.

All their winter's work had softened into a gooey mess. But Charles did not give up. In the spring of 1837, he borrowed more money and took his family back to New Haven. Then he went on alone to New York.

An old friend from Connecticut, John W. Sexton, believed Goodyear would find a solution to the rubber problem. He let him use a room in a building on Gold Street for a workshop. Still another friend who was a druggist supplied him with chemicals on credit.

In the room, with only a skylight for illumination, Goodyear experimented with raw rubber, magnesium, and quicklime. Finally, he produced a smooth, non-sticky rubber. He brought his family to Staten Island, and in a small factory there they helped him make more rubber goods. He opened a store on Broadway to sell his rubber products, and for a time the family lived in comfort.

Then Goodyear discovered his rubber could be ruined by acids such as vinegar or apple juice. People began to return their purchases and demand their money back. Once more, Goodyear was in debt and his family was hungry. But Clarissa did not lose faith. She encouraged him to keep trying.

So Charles Goodyear stuck to his purpose. In 1837,

66

Nathaniel Haywood, who had patented a process of mixing sulphur and rubber, began to work with Goodyear. The two of them experimented together, combining their methods. They finally produced a good rubber coating. Goodyear was assigned the patent for this process in 1839.

Hopefully, he sent samples to President Andrew Jackson. The government gave him an order for 150 mailbags. The Goodyear family helped make the bags, but in hot weather the heavy bags became soft and separated from their handles.

People now lost confidence in all of Goodyear's rubber goods. Many of them called him a rubber lunatic. Again and again, he was thrown into prison for debt, but he could not give up. Scornfully, his friends said he should get a regular job and support his family.

Then, in the year he received his patent, his luck changed. One day his brother, Nelson, two other men, and his daughter were in the kitchen when he accidentally dropped a lump of rubber on the hot stove. He picked it up to find it charred on the outside, but pliable and non-sticky inside.

His daughter said afterward, "An expression of ecstasy came over his face."

Charles Goodyear had discovered what became

Charles Goodyear accidentally discovering what
became known as the vulcanizing process.

known as the vulcanizing process. The word comes from the Roman god of fire, Vulcan. Vulcanizing means that under varying temperatures rubber, treated with sulphur, can produce a soft, pliable rubber, or rubber hard enough for automobile tires.

Goodyear built a brick oven to experiment with different degrees of heat to vulcanize his rubber compound. Now that success seemed certain, his brother-in-law, William deForest, lent him money. Later, he was also backed by Rider & Company of New York. After several years of testing, he finally produced a rubber that was not affected by heat or cold. He secured a patent for this vulcanizing rubber on June 14, 1844. He had been experimenting for more than ten years.

Goodyear sold licenses to rubber manufacturers. At last, he was a success. Money was coming in. He wasted much of it in his enthusiasm for rubber products, trying to make such things as rubber pianos and rubber sails.

While business was doing so well, he took his family to Europe to secure patents and establish the rubber business there. In England, he found that a man named Thomas Hancock had stolen his idea and secured the English patent. Expensive lawsuits followed, and

Goodyear lost. However, he sold some English rights to manufacturers. His earnings were enough to keep his family in luxury. He even had time to write a book: *Gum Elastic and Its Varieties.*

It the International Exhibition in London in 1851, Goodyear entered a thirty-thousand-dollar display of rubber. This was the same exhibition in which Mc-Cormick won the grand prize for his reaper in the farm display. But in spite of all his success, Goodyear still had problems to face. Both he and Clarissa were often ill while living in England. Finally, she died in March, 1853. After a lonely year, Goodyear married twenty-two-year-old Fannie Wardell of London.

The Goodyears moved to France, where Charles entered a large display of rubber goods in a Paris exhibition. Now he was able to secure patents in several European countries and sold rubber rights to manufacturers in France and Germany.

Though returns from his rubber sales should have been enough to support his family in comfort, the two expensive exhibitions plunged Goodyear into debt again. There was also a slump in his income from American rights. Once again he could not pay his debts. He was thrown into prison in France, and spent sixteen days there before Charles, Jr., could arrange his release. During that embarrassing experience, the French Emperor Napoleon III awarded him the Grand Medal of Honor for his rubber invention.

After eight years abroad, the Goodyears returned to the United States. His rubber interests in America improved, so he was able to buy a fine home in Washington, D. C. But the years of poverty and strain had broken his health. The final blow came when he learned that his daughter, Cynthia, was dying in New Haven. On his way to see her, he was taken ill in New York City and died in a hotel there on July 1, 1850.

Goodyear had struggled for years, keeping himself and his family in poverty, to solve one problem—how to make raw rubber into a useful product. He himself received little money compared with the fortunes made later by manufacturers of rubber products. But his drive and persistence made rubber a vital part of America's biggest industry—automobiles—and of many other important industries, too.

FIVE

Thomas Alva Edison

America's Greatest Inventor

BY THE TIME young Thomas Alva Edison was five, he was often getting into trouble. One day he was missing from home. His father went to look for him, and found him sitting on a nest of eggs.

"What are you doing, Al?" Mr. Edison asked.

"I'm going to hatch some eggs like the goose hatched her goslings," the boy replied.

Even at that early age he had begun his experiments. He would try anything to find out "What would happen if. . . ." Sometimes his eagerness to learn about things brought disaster. Once he started a fire inside the barn to see what would happen. He found out.

The barn burned down! His father whipped him in front of the crowd of watchers for that.

Thomas Alva Edison, who became our country's greatest electrical genius, was born on February 11, 1847, in Milan, Ohio. His parents, Nancy and Samuel Edison, also had two older children, William Pitt and Tannie.

Al was seven when his family moved to Port Huron, Michigan. He entered school there, but went only three months. The teacher thought he was not very bright.

"He's addled," she said to his mother. On hearing this, Mrs. Edison angrily took the boy home. She decided to teach him herself, for she had been a teacher before her marriage.

Al learned easily at home, and his father gave him twenty-five cents for every book he read. After a while he needed no encouragement. He had become an eager reader. He was only nine when his mother gave him a big book called Burton's *Dictionary of Science*. This book got him interested in experimenting with chemicals.

In later years Edison said, "My mother was the making of me. She understood me, and let me follow my bent."

73

He sold vegetables from his garden to earn money to buy chemicals. At first, he did his experiments in his room. To keep his family from interfering in his work, he labeled the bottles POISON. But after he spilled acids all over the rugs and furniture, his mother made him set up his laboratory in the basement.

The 1850's were exciting times for an alert boy. New steamboats and steam engines were chugging up and down rivers and across the countryside, the fastest transportation anyone had ever seen. Morse's invention of the telegraph made many boys want to learn the Morse code of dots and dashes. With his friend Michael Gates, who did chores on the farm, Al played at being a telegraph operator. He ran wires from tree to tree. Then he built a telegraph set of bottles insulated with rags, powered by a battery he bought with his vegetable money.

He wanted more money for chemicals, batteries, and other equipment. When he was twelve, he got a job as a butcher boy, selling newspapers, candy, and sandwiches on the Grand Trunk Railroad. The train left Port Huron at 7 A.M., and arrived in Detroit three hours later, then returned to Port Huron that night.

There was nothing shy about young Tom Edison. He knew how to make the most out of his new job.

Young Thomas Edison selling newspapers on a train.

In addition to selling newspapers, sandwiches, and candy, he peddled vegetables from his garden to the train crew and to people along the way. He even got permission to set up a small laboratory in one corner of the baggage car.

During the train's stopover in Detroit, Edison spent his time at the library. He was interested in newspapers as well as books, and decided to print a paper of his own. He bought a secondhand printing press, and worked on his news sheet in the baggage car. At stations along the way, he jumped off the train to sell his news sheet for a few pennies, along with the *Detroit Free Press* and his other wares. His little paper had much local news, so he generally sold all his copies.

One day, after a stop at Smith's Creek Station, Edison was trying to get back on the baggage car with his papers when the train started. The conductor reached down to help and grabbed him by the ears. Something snapped inside the boy's ears, and pain shot through his head. This accident left him partly deaf, and his hearing steadily grew worse throughout his life.

One morning, he was waiting at the St. Clemens Station while some freight cars were shifted. Suddenly he noticed the stationmaster's little boy, Jimmy Mac-Kenzie, playing on the track. The train was backing up toward the little boy. Tom dashed onto the track just in time to rescue him. Mr. MacKenzie was so grateful that he offered to teach Edison to become a telegraph operator. Tom eagerly accepted, but for a time he also continued his job on the raiload.

Not long afterward, however, he accidently set the baggage car on fire when he spilled some chemicals. Angrily, the conductor threw him and all his possessions off the train. With his job gone, young Edison

76

returned to St. Clemens. There, Mr. MacKenzie kept his promise and taught him to be a fast telegraph operator.

In the meantime, Edison's deafness was growing worse. Though he found it hard to hear everything people said, he could hear the click of the telegraph machine very well. After five months' training with Mr. MacKenzie, he was given his first job as an operator in 1863 at Stratford Junction in Canada. Sometimes he grew more interested in experimenting with the telegraph machinery than in doing his job. One day

Edison the telegrapher.

Edison's electrical vote recorder.

he was fired for neglecting his duties. But older opera-
tors were away fighting the Civil War, so it was fairly
easy for him to get another job. For five years, he was
a roving telegraph operator, going from one job to
another.

He was working as an operator in Boston, Massachusetts, when he invented the electrical vote recorder.
He was twenty-one when he applied for his first patent. He went to Washington to demonstrate the recorder to some congressmen, thinking they might find

it useful in Congress. To his surprise they did not want it. Congressmen often did not like others to know how they voted. Edison then decided he would never make another invention that was not needed.

Early in 1869, he arrived in New York, penniless, to look for a job. He contacted a friend, who lent him a dollar to buy food. Another friend, Franklin L. Pope, had an office in the Gold and Stock Telegraph Company. Pope knew of Edison's experiments in telegraphy and wanted to help him, so he arranged for Tom to sleep in the basement of the stock company building. The ever-curious Edison spent much time studying the stock tickers, machines that reported the prices of gold and other stocks. He had even made a stock ticker of his own back in Boston.

One day, stock tickers all over the building stopped running. Everyone panicked, for while the tickers were not reporting the changing prices of gold, fortunes could be lost on Wall Street, where gold and other stocks were bought and sold.

Dr. S. S. Laws, vice-president of the Gold Exchange, asked frantically if anyone knew what was wrong with the tickers. Edison, who had already been trying to find the trouble, said, "I think I can fix it."

"Then fix it! Fix it! Be quick!" urged Dr. Laws.

In about two hours, Edison repaired the damage and had all the machines operating. On learning how much this young man knew about stock tickers, and how much mechanical ability he had, Dr. Laws made him superintendent of the entire plant at a salary of three hundred dollars a month. This was considered a princely salary in those days.

Edison could scarcely believe his luck. At last, he had money to buy more materials for his experiments. His next invention was the Universal Stock Ticker, for which he received forty thousand dollars in 1870. At last, he could afford to have the laboratory and shop he had wanted all his life. He began manufacturing stock tickers in Newark, New Jersey.

Edison was free to concentrate on inventions. From his laboratory, applications for patents poured into the patent office in Washington. He helped the inventors of the typewriter, the Sholes brothers, improve their machine and make it into a successful working model. He also improved Alexander Graham Bell's telephone to make it commercially profitable.

As success came to him, Edison did not forget his aging parents. He wrote to his father, sending money, and urging him to stop working so hard.

In his days as a telegraph operator, Edison had experimented in trying to send more than one telegraph message over a wire at the same time. Now, he worked on perfecting this idea. Finally, he secured a patent for his multiplex system, by which one wire could be used for many messages. This saved the telegraph company millions of dollars.

Among the girls who worked in Edison's shop was pretty Mary Stillwell. Edison could not hear her soft voice very well, but he never let his deafness handicap him. He taught Mary the Morse code of dots and dashes. In this way, they communicated, and eventually he asked her to marry him. Mary was very patient with her genius-husband, even when he stayed at the plant all night, working on some experiment, or forgot to come home to eat.

She often packed sandwiches for him, but worried about them getting stale. So Edison invented wax paper to wrap them in.

Three years after their marriage, Edison moved his laboratory to the little village of Menlo Park, New Jersey. On a hill on the outskirts of the town he built a home for his wife and three children: a girl, Marion, and two boys, Thomas Alva and William.

Soon, he became interested in finding a way to record sounds. He experimented with a sheet of tinfoil

Other Edison Inventions

Telephone

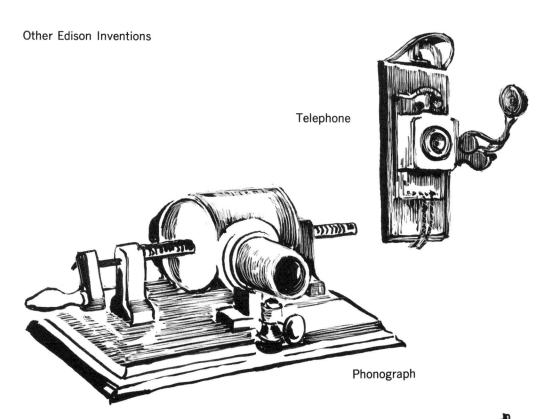

Phonograph

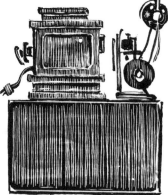

Movie Projector

wrapped around a cylinder. On the tinfoil, a recording needle made impressions of the vibrations of the human voice. Edison's experiments with telegraph instruments helped him perfect his new idea. After many failures, he finally thought he had a machine that would work.

His staff of scientists gathered around the new instrument. Edison shouted into it while turning a hand crank, "Mary had a little lamb." Then he set the needle back to the beginning of the cylinder and turned the hand crank. Back came his own voice: "Mary had a little lamb." His listeners could scarcely believe what they heard—a human voice coming out of a machine. Edison had invented the phonograph.

He applied for a patent on December 15, 1877. The invention soon made him world famous. When he demonstrated it in New York, throngs of amazed people came to hear a machine talk.

After listening, a newspaper reporter asked, "Aren't you a good deal of a wizard, Mr. Edison?"

He answered with a laugh, "Oh, no, I don't believe much in that sort of thing."

From then on he became known as the "Wizard of Menlo Park."

He spent half the next year perfecting the phonograph. After a vacation in Wyoming that summer, he returned to his laboratory to begin the most important invention of his life—the electric light.

Charles J. Brush had already invented an arc lamp, a light powered by electricity, but it was too brilliant for indoor use. When the power was cut down, the light went out. Many others had tried to invent electric lights.

After more than a thousand experiments with platinum and other wires in a vacuum tube, Edison realized he was on the wrong track. Then on October 21, 1879, he replaced the wires with a simple cotton sewing thread that had been carbonized. He bent it in a horseshoe shape in a vacuum tube and turned on the electric current. The tube gave off a glowing light. For over forty hours Edison and his assistants watched while the light still burned. At last he had succeeded! The whole world could soon be lighted by electricity.

The electric light was only the beginning of Edison's work with electricity. By December, all the streets and buildings at Menlo Park were lighted, and the public was invited to see the wonderful display.

An electric lamp factory and an electric railway to carry freight were built at Menlo Park. New York City soon had a power plant, with electric lights in buildings and on streets, replacing the old gas lamps.

84

The discovery of the electric light.

Now, the Menlo Park buildings had become too small for Edison's expanding work. So he built new shops and laboratories at West Orange, New Jersey.

During those busy years of installing electric power systems, Edison's wife died. His sons went to live with their aunt, while Marion stayed home with him as a companion and comforter.

Edison was married again, in 1886, to Nina Miller. They also had three children: Charles, Madaline, and

Theodore. The family lived on a beautiful estate called Belmont on Orange Mountain, New Jersey.

In 1891, Edison invented the motion picture camera, and a projector that enlarged the pictures. He and his co-workers experimented for five years and spent about a million dollars before perfecting the storage battery. When they worked through the night, they had supper sent in. On these occasions, the inventor relaxed and enjoyed stories and jokes with his assistants. When he was too exhausted, he climbed on his desk, put a large book under his head, and slept soundly for an hour.

On December 14, 1914, a fire broke out in a shop at West Orange. It quickly spread to other buildings and destroyed most of Edison's laboratories. But he took the fire with great calmness. He even sent for his wife and children.

"They may never see such a fire again," he said, as chemicals exploded, brightening the sky like fire-crackers.

As soon as the fire was out, he began giving orders to clear the ruins, and making plans for rebuilding.

By the time the laboratories were restored, the United States Navy was being threatened by German submarines in World War I. The Navy asked Edison to make some devices for defense against the enemy.

The inventor dropped most of his other work, and in his laboratories he and his assisting scientists served their country without pay.

During those years, Edison created over forty defensive devices. Among them were a device that warned a ship of an approaching torpedo; a light that could not be seen by a submarine; a finder for detecting airplanes. For these inventions and many others, he was awarded the Distinguished Service Medal by the Navy, the first private citizen ever to receive this honor.

By the time the war was over, Edison was very tired and his health was failing. Finally, at eighty, he turned over his business to his son Charles. The aging inventor then spent most of his time on his Florida estate, where he had a large botanical garden. He was soon experimenting again. This time, his search was for a rubber substitute, for the war had made foreign supplies of rubber very scarce. After testing thousands of plants, he finally made a substitute for rubber from a new strain of goldenrod.

This was the last of the thousands of experiments Thomas Edison carried on in his very useful life. During these fruitful years, he patented over a thousand inventions.

Honors were conferred on him from every direc-

Henry Ford and Thomas Edison.

tion. One was the celebration held in Greenfield Village at Dearborn, Michigan, in October 1929, for the fiftieth anniversay of the invention of the electric light bulb. Henry Ford, a longtime friend of Edison's, had built a replica of the old Menlo Park Laboratories for the occasion. The high point of the celebration was a banquet in Edison's honor. Famous people from all over the world attended, among them President and Mrs. Herbert Hoover. Millions of people listened over the radios that Edison had helped to create. Thousands watched while the aged inventor turned on a replica of the first electric light and said, "Let there be light." Then the whole area was flooded with light.

The strain of the day was too much for the feeble Edison. Before the banquet was over, he collapsed. After returning to his home, he lingered in failing health until October 16, 1931.

At the celebration in Dearborn, President Hoover had expressed the gratitude of all the world for this great man when he said, "Mr. Edison has repelled the darkness, and brought to our country great distinction throughout the world. He has brought benefaction to all of us."

INDEX

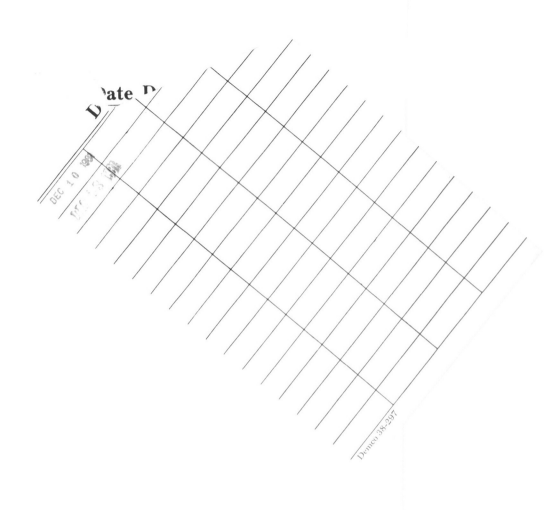

Date D

Demco 38-297